YOUR KNOWLEDGE HAS

Do Hai Dang Le

Current usage and potentials of IT-based business simulation games

GRIN Verlag

Bibliografische Information der Deutschen Nationalbibliothek:

Die Deutsche Bibliothek verzeichnet diese Publikation in der Deutschen National-
bibliografie; detaillierte bibliografische Daten sind im Internet über http://dnb.d-
nb.de/ abrufbar.

Imprint:

Copyright © 2012 GRIN Verlag GmbH
Druck und Bindung: Books on Demand GmbH, Norderstedt Germany
ISBN: 978-3-656-54215-5

This book at GRIN:

http://www.grin.com/en/e-book/264697/current-usage-and-potentials-of-it-based-
business-simulation-games

Current usage and potentials of IT-based business simulation games

12-Week Thesis in partial fulfillment of the requirements for the degree
Bachelor of Science in Business Information Systems
at the University Göttingen

submitted on 12.11.2012
by Do Hai Dang Le
from Ho Chi Minh City, Vietnam

Table of contents

List of figures

List of abbreviations

V

1. Introduction

Business simulation gaming has a long history, which can be traced back to the first simulation gaming practices in ancient China about 5.000 years ago. In modern days, the closest predecessors of modern IT-based business simulation games (IT-based BSGs) first appeared in 1932 in Europe and in 1955 in North America (cf. Faria et al. 2009, p. 465). Over the last century, IT-based BSGs have received much attention from researchers and practitioners. While many studies hitherto focus on the effectiveness and characteristics of specific games, only few have tried to review the current usage of IT-based BSGs thoroughly. In addition, the number of studies taken to evaluate the impacts of specific concepts and technologies on the future of this method is even lower. The two shortcomings in business gaming research have led to two questions, which serve as the foundations for this thesis: "How are IT-based BSGs used right now in practice?" and "How would the future of IT-based BSGs be?".

By firstly reviewing current literature on business simulation gaming and IT-based BSGs, this thesis will provide an overview on the usage of IT-based BSGs at present. After that, several selected potential concepts and technologies will be studied to discuss how they can affect the future of IT-based BSGs.

In the first chapter, before going to any of the two main questions, basic knowledge on IT-based BSGs will be provided. Additionally, the chapter also introduces their general features, the standard process of deploying them in practice and the standard architecture of current IT-based BSGs. After that, the following two chapters will answer the questions correspondingly. Chapter 3 will focus on the current usage of IT-based BSGs. Each of the application fields and the concrete usage purposes in each field will be presented. In addition, actual and relevant examples will also be presented to demonstrate them. Chapter 4 will proceed with the second question, on the potentials of specific concepts and technologies for the future development of IT-based BSGs. The chapter will be divided into two parts, with the first concentrating on the concepts and the second on the technologies. The last chapter, the discussion, will summarize and discuss the findings in the previous chapters

2. Basic knowledge

Because IT-based BSGs represent only a small subset of a wide and overarching concept of simulation gaming, this first chapter of the thesis is dedicated to provide an understanding of IT-based BSGs by starting with the definitions of simulations, games and simulation games in section 2.1. Subsequently, section 2.2 will present the general underlying features and characteristics of IT-based BSGs. Furthermore, because the term "IT-based business simulation game" can be understood both as the process of playing the games and as the systems, which people use to play the games, the standard playing process and also the standard architecture of IT-based BSGs will be introduced in section 2.3 and 2.4. The introduction of the process and the architecture is not an abundance, because both of them will be used again in chapter 4.

2.1 IT-based business simulation games

Before going to the definition of IT-based business simulation game, one has to understand the two foundations of simulation game, which are the simulation and the game. A simulation is "a representation of the reality it is constructed to depict" (Feinstein et al. 2002, p. 734). Thus, a computer simulation can be defined as an attempt to replicate the characteristics of a system by mathematics or simple object representations (cf. Feinstein et al. 2002, p. 737). Game consists of "interactions among groups of players (decision makers) placed in a prescribed setting and constrained by a set of rules and procedures" (Hsu 1989, p. 409).

Sitzmann (2011, p. 492) described several literatures which introduced games with less entertainment value and simulations with less real-world representation. Those tools inherit characteristics of both simulation and game but it is not appropriate to arrange them to either of the two categories. As a result, the term "simulation game" is the most proper to describe them (cf. Sitzmann 2011, p. 492). In general, a simulation game involves gaming activities in a simulated context and consists of four foundations: the simulation model, interaction, rules and goals. The emergence of the concept of simulation game is described in figure 1 below.

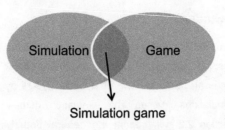

Simulation game

Figure 1: The emergence of the simulation game concept

Historically, simulation games were used exclusively for military training (cf. Faria et al. 2009, p. 465). In modern day, the use of simulation games has extended far beyond these traditional fields. The figure below describes a hierarchy of the modern application fields of simulation game.

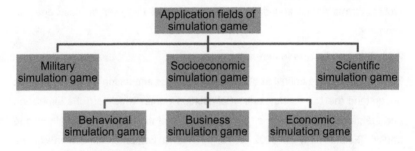

Figure 2: Modern application fields of business simulation games

Source: Kern (2003, p.83)

All of simulation game types above attempt to simulate real-life situations of the field, in which they are applied, and BSGs are no exceptions. According to Fripp (1997, p. 138), BSGs, which are also named management games or management simulation games by other authors, generally involve the representation of a real or hypothetical business environment where players can compete (cf. Fripp 1997, p. 138).

This paper focuses on IT-based BSGs that are subject to the aforementioned definition of Fripp and are constructed and deployed based on modern information and communication technologies (ICT), in contrary to early BSGs, which were either pencil-and-paper, board or card games. In the literature, there are simultaneously used terms such as "computer-based business simulation game" or "internet-based business simulation game". However, they refer to the medium in which the games are distributed and can be arranged under the overarching term "IT-based business simulation game".

2.2 General features of IT-based business simulation games

Up until now, there have been many researches taken to identify the features of simulation games and particularly IT-based BSGs. However, each of them tends to focus on one specific game with all of its technologies and subject matters to investigate its features and then generalize them to be the general features of simulation games. This method of study was considered problematic because it might not identify the underlying mechanism of simulation game (cf. Cannon-Bowers/Bowers 2008, p. 318; cf. Bell et al. 2008, p. 1418). For that reason, Bell et al. (2008, p. 1418 ff.) suggested viewing through all the embedded technologies and subject matters of specific simulation games in order to identify the underlying features. They suggested a framework that divides the underlying features of IT-based business simulations into four categories: content, immersion, interactivity and communication. In each of the categories, the features are arranged from low to high with respect to the richness of information or experience that they provide participants.

2.2.1 Content

This category describes the richness level with which basic declarative information is presented to learners (cf. Bell et al. 2008, p. 1420). Content richness increases from text, through still image, animation and video to voice.

In the past, teachers and learners used traditional instructional methods such as lecture, classroom discussion and case study and had only text and still images at their disposal. With the advancement of ICT, "richer" contents have been used increasingly in the classrooms. IT-based BSGs are no exceptions. They can utilize a wide range of instructional content. Beside those that use only text and still images, some newer IT-based BSGs use videos played by professional actors or animations coupled with audio files and play them when an in-game event takes place (cf. Summers 2004, p. 226). Moreover, experts also believe that the next generation IT-based BSGs made for young learners should also include high-quality graphics equivalent to those in video games (cf. Prensky 2001, cited in Summers 2004, p. 225).

Some studies have proven that a high degree of content richness should motivate learners and consequently increase their performance and satisfaction (cf. Kozlowski/Bell 2007, p. 26; cf. Sun/Cheng 2007, p. 12; cf. Tennyson/Jorczak 2008, p. 7).

2.2.2 Immersion

Immersion contains features that influence the sense of realism of the instructional system. Realism can be defined as "the degree of complexity that exists for a given situation and that this is related to the number of factors that surround that situation" (Micklich 1998, p. 90).

According to Bell et al. (2008, p. 1420), systems with a low level of immersion only bear little resemblance to real-life situations. Those with a medium degree of immersion such as IT-based BSGs can evoke in learners psychological processes relevant to real-life situations and provide them with the feeling of actually involving in the situations. Systems with a higher level of immersions including scientific computer simulations utilize state-of-the-art technologies such as virtual reality and three-dimensional simulation. The immersion feature of IT-based BSGs can be down to the simulation model of the game, which attempt so model a real business environment (cf. Fripp 1997, p. 138; cf. Faria et al. 2009, p. 469).

Several studies on this topic found that the benefits that immersion brings to business simulations are providing participants with realistic practical experience and engaging, as well as maintain the motivation of participants in the gaming process (cf. Bell et al. 2008, p. 1420; cf. Psotka 1995, p. 409 ff.).

2.2.3 Interactivity

According to Kozlowski/Bell (2007, p. 26), features that belong to the category "Interactivity" are those that can influence the potential degree and type of the interactions among participants and between participants and instructors. This category can be easily mistaken for the category "communication", which focuses more on the technological aspects of the games. The category "Interactivity" concerns the design factors of the games that determine whether the gaming process is centered on individual participant in isolated circumstances or on groups of participants (cf. Kozlowski/Bell 2007, p. 27).

Depending on the purpose of the course, business simulations can be designed with various degree of interactivity. According to Orth (1997, p. 20) business simulations can involve only one player, one group of players as well as multiple players or groups of players. In addition, the games may be facilitated with or without competition between participants. Furthermore, competitive games can be interactive or non-interactive, whereby in non-interactive business simulations the decisions of one player or one group have no influence over the outcomes of the decisions of others (cf. Orth 1997, p. 20).

A high degree of interactivity and competitiveness brings several benefits to IT-based BSGs. Orth (1997, p. 20) claimed that the games can promote interaction between participants and the competitiveness during game play can evoke the desire to win in learners, which consequently increases their motivation.

2.2.4 Communication

The last category contains features that influence the communication richness of the games. Unlike the previous category, this category focuses more on the technological aspects that influence the interaction among participants. Depending on the direction of flow of communication, temporal lag and transferred content, it can be differentiated between one-way and two-way, asynchronous and synchronous as well as audio and audio-visual communications, whereas in each pair, the latter contain more communication richness than the former.

IT-based BSGs can be used in combination with different communication channels with different levels of communication richness. Along with the history of business simulation, researchers have observed the use of a wide variety of communication methods at different levels of richness. Examples are e-mail and chat, forum entries, audio conferencing, Voice-over-IP protocol and even video conferencing services (cf. Fritzsche/Cotter 1992, p. 51; cf. Proserpio/Gioia 2007, p. 71; cf. Rainey/Lawlor-Wright 2011, p. 3 ff.). These communication channels can be embedded into business simulation programs as in the cases of chat and forum, or can be offered by external service provider such as e-mail and video conferencing services.

A high richness of communication can help reducing not only the spatial but also the temporal gaps between participants and allows a flexible use of IT-based business simulation game. Moreover, "richer" communication also means more detailed content can be used in the conversation (audio-visual against only audio), which makes it more understandable. This is also the point where IT-based BSGs differentiate themselves from classroom BSGs.

The aforementioned categories and the arguments have presented the general features of IT-based BSGs. Generally, IT-based BSGs utilize a wide range of content, have a mediocre level of immersion, are highly interactive and allow for a wide range of communication channels. Besides, the general benefits associated to each feature categories are also introduced. These will serve as explanations for the application fields and usage purposes of IT-based BSGs in the next chapter.

2.3   Standard process of using IT-based business simulation games

Before proceeding to study the application fields and usage purposes of IT-based BSGs in the next chapter, it is necessary to understand the process of using this method in practice. However, there is a wide variance of BSGs on the market and each user tends to facilitate the game in his own way depending on the usage purpose. Thus, it is almost impossible to list and describe all the scenarios available. For that reason, this section can only introduce a standard simulation gaming process and a typical usage scenario of IT-based BSGs.

Blötz (2008, p. 13) introduced a typical usage scenario of IT-based BSGs, which conforms to a three-phase process introduced by Orth (1997, p. 30 ff.). This scenario and the three-phase gaming process are summarized in the following figure.

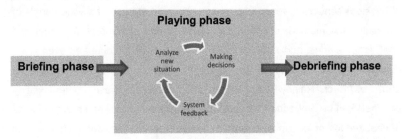

Figure 3: The standard business gaming process

Source: based on Orth (1997, p. 30 ff.) and Blötz (2008, p. 13)

In the briefing phase, participants familiarize themselves with the simulated environment of the game. Moreover, general information including the purpose, structure, rules and goals of the games will be provided. Besides, organizational preparations also take place, which typically involves the arrangement of participants typically into groups.

The playing phase is the main part of the game, which requires the most time and efforts from participants. At the beginning of the phase, participants have to analyze the starting situation and, by reference to the game goals, construct a game strategy, which sets the guidelines for later decisions. Then, after decisions are reached and submitted, they will be evaluated and their effects will be presented. Then participants will have to analyze the effects of their last decisions as well as the actualized situation to adjust their strategies and make new decisions. According to Blötz (2008, p. 13), this phase is commonly conducted in rounds, each representing a period of time in the real world.

In the debriefing phase, usually with the help of instructors, participants emerge from the game world and discuss with each other to review their experiences and impressions. Then they begin examining the simulation model, which they just played to identify the equivalence between the modeled and the real world. In the last step of the debriefing phase, they only focus on the equivalences they already identified and consider which experiences to be relevant to them and will be kept and applied after the course (cf. Steinwachs 1992, p. 187).

Although the described scenario is the most commonly used one, in practice, many of its aspects can be varied. For instance, there are games that do not require participants to be present at the same place to play. There are also games, in which participants can play individually without any interaction or competition with other peer players. The role, which participants take during game play, can also be different. Examples are functional BSGs such as stock market games, in which participants take the role of stock exchange investors, or games that focuses on the training of specific job skills. In addition, the gaming process need not necessarily be divided into rounds. Real-time BSGs such as the stock exchange game previously introduced require learners to react continuously in a continuous game play. Finally, human instructors are not necessary for some kinds of BSGs either. A more detailed understanding of all the practical usage scenarios can only be provided by studying the classifications of BSGs thoroughly.

2.4 Standard architecture of IT-based business simulation games

Beside the gaming process, the standard architecture of current IT-based BSGs should also be introduced to provide fundamental knowledge for the study of the potentials in the next chapter.

On his website, Hall (2012) summarized his experience in developing BSGs and provided a standard architecture, which is shown below.

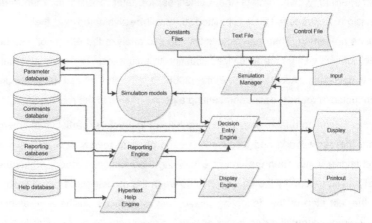

Figure 4: A standard architecture of IT-based business simulation games

Source: Hall (2012)

As shown in the figure, the simulation manager controls the interaction between the systems and users. It receives input data and controls which data will be displayed and printed out for users. The control file defines the operation of the simulation manager while the constants file and text file are used by the simulation manager to control the operation of the engines. The decision entry engine receives user input from the simulation managers, checks their validity and displays comments on the inputs if they are wrong. If the inputs are valid, they will be forwarded to the simulation models to be calculated or to the reporting engine to be displayed back to users. The reporting and hypertext help engines use data from the reporting and help databases to generate reports or helps and send them to the display engine to be displayed or printed out. The core of the architecture is the simulation model, which uses data from

9

the parameter database and input data from users to calculate the results. The result will then be sent back to the decision entry engine, which will adds comment and sends to the reporting engine to generate full reports. The reports will lastly be sent to the display engine to be displayed or printed out.

The standard architecture of IT-based BSGs marks the end of the first chapter, which has provided the basic knowledge on IT-based BSGs. The next chapter will proceed with the first topic of the thesis about how IT-based BSGs are currently used.

3. Current usage of IT-based business simulation games

The first BSGs in modern day were developed to serve the purpose of education (cf. Faria et al. 2009, p. 465). Up until now, although changes in ICT, business and educational methodology have altered BSGs, education and training still remain as the main usage purposes (cf. Orth 1997, p. 12). Beside education and training, in the literature, researchers have mentioned two other application fields of IT-based business simulations, which are experimental research and business practice (cf. Baume 2009, p. 149 ff.).

Although the application fields are different, based on a definition of computerized BSGs of Sitzmann (2011, p. 492), it can be supposed that, independent from the particular usage purposes, IT-based BSGs are deployed when facilitators need to motivate participants and to provide them with a realistic environment to create better results. According to section 2.2, depending on each game, IT-based BSGs may promote interactive and flexible learning as well. However, the motivation and realism and, above all, the ability of offering all the characteristics at the same time make IT-based BSGs a superior tool in each of the application fields. For instance, in education and training, traditional instructional methods such as class discussions and case studies can provide interaction and even flexibility if used with e-learning technologies. However, when playing IT-based BSGs, learners are motivated and continue playing until they finish the game and can even replay the game until they obtain the learning objectives. Moreover, by learning and training in a realistic environment, learners will receive realistic experiences, which make their obtained knowledge and skills closer to the requirements of the real-world business. Thus, learners will be readier for the business in the future. In both experimental research and business practice, in comparison to research and assessment methods such as laboratory experiments, surveys and tests, a motivating method will firstly help keeping participants taking part in the game till the end. Furthermore, a realistic environment may encourage participants to behave as expected in real situations, which help gathering more reliable data in case of research and revealing the real knowledge and abilities of participants in case of assessment.

In the following sections, all of the reported application fields, as well as the particular usage purposes in each field will be presented. Moreover, the advantages of IT-based BSGs in each usage purpose will also be subsequently introduced to show why practitioners have chosen to used IT-based BSGs for that purpose.

3.1 IT-based business simulation games in education and training

In education and training, IT-based BSGs are used to provide the target groups with certain knowledge and skills. The term "education and training" already shows the two different settings, in which instructional IT-based BSGs are currently deployed. While the word "education" refers to the teaching and learning process in academic institutes such as schools and universities, the word "training" has been used almost exclusively for businesses. In businesses, the target group of IT-based BSGs varies from trainees through normal employees to senior and junior managers (cf. Pivec et al. 2003, p. 222). Meanwhile, in academic institutes, the main target group is certainly students, independent from the degree they are pursuing (cf. Hauke et al. 2006, p. 13).

Combining all the teaching and training purposes in the aforementioned settings, Hauke et al. (2006, p. 36 ff.) identified four particular teaching and training purposes of IT-based BSGs, which are the teaching of basic knowledge and the interrelationships within the business as well as the training of technical skills and social skills. However, in practice, these usage purposes do not receive equal attentions from practitioners. The same study of Hauke et al. founded that both academic institutes and businesses have considered the teaching of the interrelationships and the training of social skills as more important than the other two purposes (cf. Hauke et al. 2006, p. 36 ff.).

Moreover, it should be added that the usage purposes are not mutually exclusive. In practice, there are also games developed and deployed to target multiple purposes at the same time. For example, the developers of the Capsim business simulation game declared that their game could simultaneously improve learners' basic knowledge on business operations, their financial skills and their understanding of the integration among business units, as well as their social skills such as communication, team work and leadership (cf. CAPSIM 2012).

3.1.1 Teaching basic knowledge

Knowledge, according to the widely accepted classification of learning outcomes proposed by Kraiger et al. (1993, p. 312 ff.), is categorized into three stages, which have to be achieved successively. Declarative knowledge refers to facts and data required to complete a task (the "what"). Procedural knowledge refers to knowledge about how to perform a task (the "how"). Strategic knowledge is the application of learned knowledge in different contexts and situations and the derivation of more knowledge for general situation (the "which, when, why") (cf. Garris et al. 2002, p.456).

While traditional methods focus only on declarative and procedural knowledge, there are beliefs that BSGs in general are excel at teaching higher levels of knowledge as well as improving knowledge retention. These beliefs are not groundless. The Interactive Cognitive Complexity theory of Tennyson/Jorczak (2008, p. 7) suggests that simulation games should produce better knowledge gains, because they allow the interaction between learners' affects and knowledge base. The process may be stiffened by the motivational effectiveness of IT-based BSGs, the interactivity during game play and the realistic experience provided by the games. Meta-analyses of several authors have found evidences favoring BSGs at lower knowledge levels (cf. Sitzmann 2011, p. 508; cf. Randel et al. 1993, p. 263 ff.). However, due to a lack of evaluation methods in this domain, there are only empirical evidences of the effectiveness on declarative procedural knowledge and knowledge retention (cf. Anderson/Lawton 2009, p. 200 ff.; cf. Sitzmann 2011, p. 508; cf. Wilson et al. 2009, p. 235).

3.1.2 Teaching cross-functional understanding within the business

According to Baume (2009, p. 153), many BSGs on the market require learners to play at the role of the managers of an entire company and make decisions concerning different business functions. While playing these games, learners have to apply their obtained knowledge to make decisions and then observe the impacts of the decisions on the company at a whole. The process is strengthened by the "trial and error" learning principle of BSGs, which allows learners to try making decisions and observe the results repetitively. As a consequent, learners will gain and improve their understanding of the interrelationships between business functions of the company and train their cross-functional and systematic thinking.

In practice, this usage purpose is promoted by the use of total management simulation games, with or without an emphasis on a concrete business function. In total enterprise business games, participants have to make cross-functional decisions concerning most of the main functions of a business such as research and development, procurement, production, marketing, finance and personnel (cf. Keys/Biggs 1990, p. 49). With an emphasis on a business function, the games also require learners to make decisions in other functions of the business, but tend to focus particularly on one function, making the number of decisions concerning this function more complex than others (cf. Keys/Biggs 1990, p. 49). Examples of these games are "TOPSIM General Management" and "Markstrat". While TOPSIM covers all the mentioned business functions, participants playing Markstrat focus more on the principles of marketing (cf. StratX 2012; cf. TOPSIM 2012, p. 1).

3.1.3 Training technical skills

Skill is the improvement in task performance. The process of acquiring a skill is divided into three successive stages, which can be achieved only by continuous training (cf. Garris et al. 2002, p. 455; cf. Kraiger et al. 1993, p. 317). Initial skill acquisition begins with the process of transforming declarative knowledge to procedural knowledge, in which learners learn how to perform a task. Skill compilation involves practicing trained behaviors and allows faster performance with less error. Skill automaticity enables not only a quick but also personalized performance of the tasks.

Business simulation game allows learners to repetitively practice on solving and performing a task in a realistic environment, which is a prerequisite to the obtainment and improvement of skills. Moreover, this process becomes more effective under the influence of other characteristics of IT-based BSGs such as motivational engagement and interactivity, which helps engage and maintain trainees' motivation during the game, and flexibility, which allows for a flexible and convenient learning condition. For that reason, it is reasonable to understand why practitioners have chosen this instructional method to practice technical skills.

One example for this usage purpose is the game used in the study of Léger (2006), in which participants were required to play a BSG in combination with the SAP R/3 enterprise resource planning software. Among other objectives of this simulation game, which are the teaching of knowledge relevant to the enterprise resource planning concept and the cross-functional role of the concept, the game also intend to train learners the skills of using SAP R/3 software (cf. Léger 2006, p. 4). In addition, there are also evidences of the use of simulation games to train effectively specific job skills such as personnel administration, hiring, motivating, leading or research and data analysis (cf. Faria 2001, p. 103).

3.1.4   Training social skills

The last but not less important usage purpose of IT-based business simulation in education and training setting is the training of social skills. Social skills involve the attitude toward other people and the ability to interact with them in a social context. Like technical skills, social skills can also be trained by continuously practicing. Common BSGs require learners to play in groups. Once assigned to a group, participants are required to solve specific business problems in a simulated environment together. Although both the environment and the problems are simulated, during the process, many real social problems may arise that need to be solve in order for the groups to continue playing and achieve their desired goals. By doing so, they get themselves acquainted to the real-life process of interacting with other people, which consequently improve their social skills.

In practice, there are claims of positive effects on social skills such as leadership, conflict management, communication and teamwork during participation in team-played games (cf. Greenblat 1973, p. 67; cf. Whitton/Hynes 2006; cf. Faria 2001, p. 103; cf. Arias-Aranda/Bustinza-Sánchez 2009, p. 1106).

3.2 IT-based business simulation games in experimental research

The idea of using BSGs as a research tool is not new. Actually, developers have thought of using them for research purpose as soon as they started to use them for education and training purpose (cf. Cohen/Rhenman 1961, p. 158). The general goal of the usage is to obtain empirical data, create hypotheses and analyze the data to test the hypotheses (cf. Baume 2009, p. 149). While conducting researches using BSGs, researchers profit from their characteristics. For instance, since IT-based BSGs are intrinsically motivating, participants can be kept motivated during their participation in the researches, which also increase the results of the researches. Additionally, the realism of the simulated environment provided in the games also ensures the validity of the research outcomes. Finally yet not less importantly, the controllability of the environment allows researchers to vary the environment to fit to their research purposes.

Since the 1960s, several possible research fields for BSGs were first suggested (cf. Cohen/Rhenman 1961, p. 158 ff.). Some of them were actually reviewed and confirmed by and Keys/Wolfe in their study in the 1990s (cf. Keys/Wolfe 1990, p. 318 ff.). In general, the usage of IT-based BSGs circles around three main purposes: economic research, organizational and leadership study and psychological research. In the following sections, these purposes will be further explained and illustrated by practical examples. The examples are chosen based on their actuality and their representativeness to the usage purpose.

3.2.1 Economic research

The first research field of IT-based BSGs is to provide empirical data to analyze economic theories. Because BSGs commonly involve teams playing as competing firms in a simulated, realistic environment, the whole system resembles a real economic environment and makes it possible to be used in economic researches. More particularly, Cohen/Rhenman (1961, p. 161) suggested that in the environment created in BSGs, there are a limited number of competing firms, which have the same initial state and are aware of the consequences of their decisions to each other. This environment represents an olipology. For that reason, BSGs should provide a proper method to conduct experiments in oligopoly research.

One example is a study on olipologistic pricing conducted by Sauaia/Kallás (2003). In the study, participants were required to play the computer-based business simulation "Multinational Management Game". Participants were divided into groups, with each taking the management role of a company. During game play, they had to make decisions relevant to the production and marketing of the products and the financial structure of their own company. At the end of the game, researchers collected and analyzed several key figures of teams to draw conclusions on this economic phenomenon.

3.2.2 Organizational and leadership study

The second research field that uses IT-based BSGs is organizational and leadership study. Business simulation games can be used to analyze the effects of changes of organizational structure or communication patterns on behaviors and performance, which, according to Cohen/Rhenman (1961, p. 163 f.), they can accomplish more effectively than traditionally used laboratory experiments. The reason is the close resemblance of the environment in the BSGs to the reality. Moreover, because the environment is controllable, by varying variables such as team size, team structure, time pressure and the amount information given to team members while playing the game, researchers can observe and study the effects of such independent variables on dependent results such as team behavior, performance, moral and adaptability to changes.

One concrete and actual example of this usage purpose is a study taken by Siewiorek/Lehtinen (2011) on leadership in a competing situation. The game used in the study was competitive but non-interactive computerized business simulation game, which means groups were to play the game independently and the group with the highest score at the end would win the game. Participants were divided into groups without any assignment of a leadership role. The groups were also arranged with differences in sex to create different samples. Time pressure was placed onto the game to accelerate the gaming process and increase the pressure for the emergence of a leader in the teams.

In such a situation, researchers could observe the behaviors of participants to identify which kind of leadership styles would emerge in an organization in such situation and what could be exercised by playing BSGs.

3.2.3 Psychological research

The last research field mentioned by the authors is psychological research. Because BSGs place individuals and groups under problem solving situations, it is possible to observe and study several psychological learning and problem solving behaviors (Cohen/Rhenman 1961, p. 165). Additionally, BSGs may be a more proper tool for such studies than simple games and exercises, because they provide a realistic environment, as well as a better control of the external threats and the in-game decision-making process (cf. Keys/Wolfe 1990, p. 320).

An actual example for this research field is a study taken by Bernard/Cannon in 2011. In the study, participants took part in a team-played competitive and interactive computerized business simulation game. After each round, they were asked to take a survey describing their level of motivation before and after the decision-making process. The same surveys were also taken at the beginning and the end of the course. The result would be analyzed study the patterns of their motivation throughout the game.

3.3 IT-based business simulation games in business practice

Beside the usage in education and training and experimental research, IT-based BSGs are also reported in business practice in the strategic planning and human resource management units. More particularly, in these units, the games are used to forecast the outcomes of strategies and support the decision-making process or to evaluate applicants, assess employees and promote the image of the company to potential applicants (cf. Baume 2009, p. 149; cf. Orth 1997, p. 13 f.).

3.3.1 Forecasting in strategic planning

The usage of IT-based BSGs in this setting is similar to that of the scenario method for strategic planning, in which they can be used to calculate the outcomes of different business strategies (cf. Baume 2009, p. 149). A comparison of these outcomes can support the strategic decision-making process within the company. Hauke et al. (2006, p. 40) also stated that because the parameters of the games can be adjusted to match the actual situation of the company and the time represented in the game can be accelerated or compressed when necessary, the games should provide a proper forecasting tool.

However, the actual usage of IT-based BSGs for this purpose it unclear because Karczewski (1990, p. 33) stated that when IT-based are used in this setting, the role of human during the simulation process fades into the background and the tools used should be regarded as pure computer simulations instead of simulation games. An evidence for this statement is a study of Bielecki (1993, p. 60 ff.), which suggested a method to use a modified BSG as a decision support system. The resulted system of the study contains only two main components, which are the simulation model of the initial simulation game and a database that is based on the actual database of the firm. The system would be used to answers the questions of the strategic planning process: "What is...?", "What will be...?", "What if...?", "What is best...?" and "What is good enough...?" (cf. Bielecki 1993, p. 62). The system requires only human input at the beginning of the simulation process, which clearly shows that it has lost its characteristic of a "simulation game" and may be recognized only as a "computer simulation".

3.3.2 Employee assessment and recruitment marketing

The second usage of business simulation games in business practice is the use of IT-based BSGs as a tool in the human resource unit to fulfill objectives such as evaluating applicants, assessing employees and marketing recruitment. For evaluation and assessment purposes, applicants or employees can be required to play BSGs while their behaviors and performance are evaluated (cf. Karczewski 1990, p. 34). More particularly, by placing applicants under a simulated business situation provided by BSGs, the recruiters can evaluated whether the applicants have the required knowledge and skills for the applied position. In terms of employee development, Thornton/Cleveland (1990, p. 191) suggested that the use of BSGs can provide information on the training needs of an employee or an organization and on the managerial potentials of any employee. Especially, the authors also stated that this method seems to be advantageous because there are skills and abilities that simple tests cannot identify and evaluate.

As for recruitment marketing, small and simple BSGs can be used in recruitment offices to introduce about the company or the industry and also identify potential talents. Gardner et al. (2009, p. 227) reported the use of a computerized BSG by a university in the USA to introduce middle school students to principles and carriers in supply chain management, manufacturing and logistics through a summer program. The target of this program was to grow interest from those students so that the university can receive more applicants for its offered degree in supply chain management.

To conclude this chapter and also the first topic of the thesis, it can be summarized that IT-based BSGs have been currently used in education and training, in experimental research and in business practice. However, education and training remain as the main application field with a wide variance of usage purposes. The use of BSGs in experimental research and especially business practice is limited. The type of game used in these application fields is not necessarily IT-based and even not simulation game as in the case of strategic forecasting.

4. Potentials of IT-based business simulation games

After finishing the first topic of the thesis on the present state of IT-based BSGs, this chapter will proceed with the second topic on the potentials for enhancing the performance of IT-based business simulation games in the future.

In the literature, researchers have mentioned several concepts and technologies that can affect the either the simulation gaming process or the BSG systems or both of them. However, due to the limitations of this thesis and a high number of potentials, it is not possible to study all of them. For that reason, this thesis will exemplarily select and study two concepts and two technologies to show how these two groups can affect the future of IT-based BSGs. Another criteria, which play an important role in the selection of the topics of this chapter, is the four categories, content, immersion, interactivity and communication, around which all the features and characteristics of IT-based BSGs concentrate, as introduced in section 2.3. The selected concepts and technologies should also concentrate around these four categories. Moreover, the selected concepts and technologies should be those that have not received much attention from researchers in spite of being mentioned in the literature as potentials.

A thorough literature research has found four topics, which satisfy the aforementioned selection criteria. The serious game concept is an education and training technique by itself and emphasizes the transfer of learning material while using high quality graphics and multimedia contents of video games. For that reason, it is selected for the category "content". The role-playing concept provides learners with a new and higher level of interactivity to create better experiences. Thus, this concept is selected to represent the category "interactivity", although it may also affect the degree of immersion of the games. The real-time data technology is selected for "immersion" because of its ability to provide place learners into an environment with a realistically continuous game play. The dialog system technology is merely a technology that can influence the interaction among participants. Thus, it is chosen for the category "communication". Because of the difference in the levels of the topics, between the concepts and the technologies, this chapter will be divided into two parts. The first parts will study the concepts, while the second will study the technologies.

4.1 Potentials concepts for IT-based business simulation games

In the following sections, the potential of integrating two selected concepts of serious game and role-playing into IT-based BSGs will be studied. In each topic, first, the corresponding concept will be introduced. Then, there will be a comparison between the concept and IT-based BSGs to see if they fit to each other. After that, a method for the integration will be proposed and the specific usage of the integration and the associating benefits and issues will also be introduced. In addition, since serious game is a concept that is more relevant to the technical architecture of IT-based BSGs while the role-playing concept is relevant to the gaming process, the comparisons between them and IT-based BSGs will be different.

4.1.1 The serious game concept

Like IT-based BSGs, serious game is also a newly born concept of using games in education and training. Although the term "serious game" was firstly mentioned in the literature in the 1970s, it has not been received much attention of researchers and practitioners until the widespread of computers and the emergence of computer games. Recently, several experts are urging for such integration (cf. Faria, et al. 2009, p. 470; cf. Summers 2004, p. 225). Hall (2009, p. 132) also claimed that serious game is an emergent design movement of business simulation game. However, there have been few researches taken to study thoroughly the relationships between the two concepts and the potentials of integrating both of them. For that reason, after introducing serious game, this section will provide a comparison between the architectures of the two concepts to emphasize their relationships to each other. Subsequently, the benefits and issues accompanying the integration will also be assessed.

4.1.1.1 Introduction to the serious game concept

Similar to the definition of simulation game, the definition of serious game also consist of two parts, the "serious" and the "game" part. Section 2.1 has presented a definition and characteristics of "game". People have known of games as an entertaining, enjoyable and fun way to pass time and interact with other people (cf. Micheal/Chen 2006). However, the first idea of using game for purposes other than entertainment can be traced back to Abt in his book with the same name published in 1970 and reprinted in 1987 (cf. Abt 1987, p. 9). Since the book was first published in the time when computer game did not exist, the author referred to the usage of games in general. This is neither the focus of most authors currently nor the focus of this section of the thesis. The term "serious game" nowadays can be defined as "games that make use of computer technology and advanced video graphics and that are used for the purposes of learning and training" (Crookall 2010, p. 905). This means, serious games are video games that are used for purposes other than entertainment.

Because of the definition, the architectures of serious games can be comparable to those of video games. For that reason, a standard architecture of video games can be used to represent the architecture of serious games.

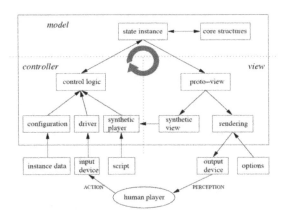

Figure 5: Architecture of a computer game

Source: Smed/Hakonen (2003, p. 4)

The figure above describes a model-view-controller architecture of video game suggested by Smed/Hakonen (2003, p. 4). Accordingly, the model is the center of the game, which consists of a core structure that stores rules and basic entity information and a state instance that changes during the game process to represent the actual state of the game. The view component consists of a proto-view that receives information and data from the model and illustrates them in the synthetic view for synthetic players (the computer players) or sends them through the rendering component to display to human players. The controller is made up of a driver that receives player input, a configuration that defines the initial state of the game and synthetic players. Data from these components are sent to the control logic to affects the state instance of the model. In video games and particularly serious games, the view component is emphasized with the used of multimedia contents and high quality graphics.

Originally developed for the military, the usage of serious game has extended to other application fields. However, the application fields of serious games intersect with those of IT-based BSGs only at business education and training (cf. Micheal/Chen 2006, p. 46 f.). The first serious video game for business training was developed in the early 1980s. Newer examples include games such as NoviCraft HRD and Heroes of Industry. NoviCraft HDR is a game developed in 2008, which place participants in real-life situations to teach the importance of issues such as communication, leading, coordination and goal orientation (cf. NoviCraft 2012). The aim of the game is to increase employees' team working and leadership skills. Meanwhile, Heroes of Industry was developed in 2006 with the purpose of teaching new employees of the transports and logistic industry the basic knowledge on tasks including sorting and packaging dangerous goods, documenting and recording movements of goods, identifying suspicious packages and dealing with potential security threats (cf. Simulated Training Systems 2012).

4.1.1.2 Serious game and IT-based business simulation games

When compared to the standard architecture of IT-based BSGs provided in section 2.4, it can be recognized that both have the many similarities in the architecture: the model that executes calculations, the controller that controls the flow of data in the program and the view components that controls the input and output of data. Consequently, the integration of the serious game concept to IT-based BSGs is technically possible. According to Pomper et al. (2009, p. 3) serious games focuses more on the view component by using high-quality graphic and multimedia content while and simulation games emphasize the model to make the games more realistic. This difference appears to be the main boundary between the two concepts. To blur the boundary, propositionally, current IT-based BSGs can be redesigned with high quality graphics or current serious games and videos can be modified to make their simulation model more realistic. The results of the processes are the same, which is an instructional method that has the realism of simulation game and the high quality graphic and multimedia content of serious game. Actually, in practice, there are already incentives from both sides. From the side of business simulation game, experts believe that future business simulations should also include high-quality graphics equivalent to those in video games (cf. Prensky 2001 cited in Summers 2004, p. 225). Meanwhile, from the side of serious game, Pomper et al. (2009, p. 3) also mentioned that serious game developers frequently use simulation techniques in their games to create a certain level of immersion needed to fulfill the educational goals of the games, which partially blurs the boundary between the two concepts. The examples of serious games given in section 4.1.1.1 also show that currently used serious game also have several points of resemblance to BSGs in which they all try to represent real-life situations to some extents.

4.1.1.3 Usage, benefits and issues

Micheal/Chen (2006, p. 155 f.) cited Prensky (2001) and claimed that serious games can be useful in situations when the learning material is dry or boring, when the learning objectives are too complex, when the target group is difficult to reach, when sophisticated consequence analysis is required, and when communicating or developing corporate strategies. Thus, the integration of serious games and IT-based BSGs might also be useful in these cases. The graphical user interface of the game Markstrat, which uses only text, can be taken as an example. The game is a common IT-based BSG that was already mentioned in section 3.1.2. This can be regarded as the point where "the material is dry or boring" and where the integration of the serious game concept might be promising. Integrating the serious game concept to this BSG may require the complete redesign of the display engine of the game. For example, instead of presenting the business units and their functions in program tabs by using only pieces of text, the entire company could be visualized with video game graphic as a group of buildings, with each represents a business unit. When users click on one of the buildings, the contents of the corresponding unit would be opened. Inside each of the units, the contents would also be visualized differently from the original. By doing so, it is reasonable to believe that the integration would make the game more interesting for learners. The reason is that serious games and IT-based BSGs both share the characteristics of "game" and consequently the main benefit of the application of gaming in education and training, which is the ability to motivate, engage and maintain learners' attention (cf. de Freitas 2006, p. 12).

However, to a specific group of learners, the integration may show additional benefits. A survey in 2007 revealed that 40 percent of the German population was playing video games at that time (cf. Hottner 2007, p. 4). In addition, it can be assumed that these video gamers, whom Proserpio/Gioia (2007, p. 70) called "the virtual generation", will become future students and trainees and target groups of business education and training. Virtual technologies including video game have transformed the learning style of this generation so that they now preferred the immersive experiences, to which they have been accustomed in video games, to traditional methods (cf. Proserpio/Gioia 2007, p. 73). And since Proserpio/Gioia (2007, p. 69) claimed that the teaching style have to conform the learning style in order to enhance the learning process, it is reasonable to think that video game is a proper teaching method for students and trainees of this generation. Micheal/Chen (2006, p. 26) also agreed with this by stating that since this generation of students and trainees are used to video games, they would be more likely to prefer playing video games and learning from video games.

However, the integration also leads to various issues that need to be attended. Although the integration described exemplarily with the game Markstrat is possible as in the example, it may also make the game development more costly and complicated. Moreover, the deployment of the game in reality may also be problematic, with regard to the hardware required to render the graphic of the game. Besides, de Freitas (2006, p. 18) and Micheal/Chen (2006, p. 160 ff.) also express concerns on the context of usage and the element of fun of the games. Although there is a high number of video gamers in the population, which leads to an expectation of the success of serious game, there are people who do not know video games, and do not like playing video games either (cf. de Freitas 2006, p. 19). If forced to play video games, this group will not ensure the effectiveness of the games. This problem resembles a similar problem in game-based learning methods identified by Wawer et al. (2010, p. 66) and Wong et al. (2007, p. 56). The authors suggested that the unfamiliarity with the concept and the technologies might increase the time required for learners to get used to the games and consequently reduce the learning effectiveness of the games. For that reason, there have to be thorough considerations before choosing whether to use video game for the training course.

To conclude this section, it can be summarized that the architectures of serious game and IT-based BSGs are similar, which make an integration of the two concepts possible. However, while the application of video game design to IT-based BSGs may promise a higher level of effectiveness to a certain segment of the virtual generation, the video gamers, it may also cause additional problems. For that reason, applying video game design to IT-based BSGs should not be considered as an obligation, but only an option to facilitators, who wish to adapt their method to meet with the new generation.

4.1.2 The role-playing concept

After finishing with the first concept, this section will proceed with the role-playing concept. As it will be explained further in this section, this concept focuses on the interaction between learners. In addition, although this concept and its usage in education and training are not new and despite the similarities between both of them, there have been few researches conducted to study the relationship between this concept and IT-based BSGs.

In the following sections, first, an introduction on the role-playing concept will provide basic information on its definition, characteristics and usage. Second, since role-playing and IT-based business simulation are equally comparable concepts in education and training, two concepts will be compared to see whether they are fit to each other and a propositional method to integrate role-playing to the business gaming process. Last, the usage, as well as the advantages and issues of the integration will be discussed.

4.1.2.1 Introduction to the role-playing concept

Like both the definitions of simulation game and serious game, the term "role-play" also consists of two parts: role and play. Role in a social context is "a socially prescribed way of behaving in particular situations for any person occupying a given social position or status" (cf. Coutu 1951, p. 180). From the definition of role, authors mentioned several features contributing to a definition of role-playing. Accordingly, role-playing requires participant to "pretend to play a role" while "interacting with other role-player", who are also "constrained by a set of conditions" and "in a simulated situation" (cf. Coutu 1951, p. 181 f.; cf. Feinstein et al. 2002, p. 735; cf. Linser 2011, p. 908; cf. Wills/McDougall 2009, p. 762).

In practice, van Ments (1983, p. 51 f.) described a typical process of role-playing, which resembles the five-phase learning design of online role-playing proposed by Wills/McDougall (2009, p. 768). First, participants are assigned the role that they are to play at (enrole) and provided with information about the role, the case and the rules of the role-playing (research). After that, they have to communicate with other role-players who may be relevant and important to their own role (react). Later, they will be put through a series of situations with a succession of problems, which they have to negotiate with each other to solve

26

while playing the role they were assigned (resolve). After the role-play, a debriefing facilitated by an instructor will help them analyzing their behaviors and reflecting them to real-life situations (reflect). The process is summarized in the following figure.

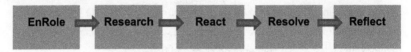

Figure 6: The role-playing process

Source: based on Wills/McDougall (2009, p. 768)

In education and training, the usage of role-playing centers on the central benefits of motivating leaners and providing them with a risk-free and psychologically realistic environment to practice. First, role-playing provides participants with realistic experiences and allows them to practice their skills by reflecting psychological and behavioral patterns, which they can expect in real-life situation (cf. van Ments 1983, p. 24). Second, the active participation and engagement in role-playing sessions may also improve and maintain learners' motivation level, which may consequently improve their learning outcomes and retention (cf. Sogunro 2004, p. 355 f.). Last, in role-playing, learners' emotions can be expressed freely without causing consequences on other peer players (cf. van Ments 1983, p. 24). Because of the benefits and the emphasis of role-playing on learners' interactions, in business education and training, role-playing has been used to practice interpersonal skills, group dynamics and decision-making (cf. Thiagarajan 1996, cited in Sogunro 2004, p. 357; cf. van Ments 1983, p. 27). Feinstein et al. (2002, p. 735) also stated that regardless of the explicit purpose, the implicit purpose of every role-play is to enhance interpersonal skills.

4.1.2.2 Role-playing and IT-based business simulation games

In comparison to the gaming process of IT-based BSGs described in section 2.3, the process of role-playing as described in the previous section show several similarities. The combination of the "enrole" and "research" phases of the role-playing process is similar to the briefing phase of the simulation gaming process, when learners receive organizational preparation and general information. The "react" and "resolve" phases are similar to the playing phase of

IT-based BSGs, where the main activities take place. The "reflect" phase is also comparable to the debriefing phase of IT-based BSGs. Furthermore, within the playing phase, participants also have to solve the problems successively. In addition, the simulation gaming process also has a degree of role-playing, in which participants or groups may have to play at the role of the top management of a company and team members have to interact with each other to make decisions (cf. Feinstein et al. 2002, p. 737). Last but not less importantly, both two concepts have been regarded to be good at providing learners with realistic experience and are used to improve learners' skills. While BSGs emphasizes the reality provided by the simulation model, the realism of role-playing is given by the representation of real-life psychological and behavioral patterns.

Because of the similarities mentioned above, it is possible to propose a framework to integrate the role-playing concept into IT-based business simulation game. Additionally, since role-playing focuses on the interaction of participants in the playing process, the two main phases of the role-playing should also be integrated to the simulation gaming process where the interaction takes place the most, which is also the playing phase of the simulation gaming process. Combining this argument and the similarity in the playing process of role-playing and business simulation game, a propositional framework for the integration is described in the figure below and will be explained further in the following paragraph.

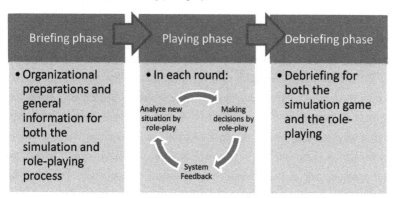

Figure 7: A propositional framework for the integration of role-playing in IT-based business simulation games

An example can be made to describe the proposed framework. In the briefing phase, participants receive organizational preparations such as group and role assignment and general information on the role and on the simulation game. In each round of the playing phase, the group members have to analyze the situation and make decisions while acting at the role they were assigned. A change of roles after each round may be considered to help participants get used to each of the different roles of the business management. In the debriefing phase, instructors help participants reflecting on their performance results and on their role behaviors during game play to improve both their cognitive learning and their managerial skills. The framework is not limited only to the described scenario. For example, in individual-played BSG with the computer playing as the opponent, role-playing can also be used, in which both the human and computer player are assigned roles to interact with each other.

4.1.2.3 Usage, benefits and issues

Since the role-playing concept focuses on the interaction between players, as long as there are interactions between participants and roles to be played at, the proposed framework can be applied. Moreover, since the target of role-playing is the training of interpersonal skills as stated by Feinstein et al. (2002, p. 735), the integration should be used in courses that, among other purposes, also focus on the training of interpersonal skills by promoting interaction among participants. An example is a course that uses the aforementioned "TOPSIM General Management" game to target not only the teaching of the interrelationships within the company but also the training of social skills. The course also involves the interaction between participants, who are arranged into groups. The game is a total enterprise business game, which requires participants to make decisions relevant to equally every business units of a company: research and development, procurement, production, sales and distribution, finance and accounting and human resource. Because the game targets all the areas equally, it might be useful and interesting to have groups made up of students from different majors and have them taking the management role of the business unit relevant to their major. By doing so, participants would obtain knowledge focusing on their major and also understand the role of their major in the entire company. More importantly, however, they might receive experiences, which are more realistic and more

29

relevant to their major than those that they might obtain when playing IT-based BSGs without any role assignment. As a result, it is reasonable to assert that the integration of the role-playing concept into the process of playing IT-based BSGs in the right situation might additionally enhance the effectiveness of IT-based BSGs.

Although it is possible and beneficent, the integration also accompanies several issues. Van Ments (1983, p. 27) mentioned some issues concerning the use of role-playing in education and training. Other authors when writing about IT-based BSGs and BSGs in genera also addressed the same issues. These include concerns on the quality of instructors during game play and in the debriefing, the unfamiliarity with the method and the seriousness of participants, the simplification of the reality and the high consumption of time and resources (cf. Hofstede et al. 2010, p. 834 ff.; cf. Wawer et al. 2010, p. 66; cf. Wellington/Faria 1992, p. 111). Since both concepts have the same problems, it is reasonable to assert that the integration not only does not help eliminating the problems but can even severe some of them. One example is the problem of time and workload consumption. Business simulation gaming has been considered as a time-consuming learning method. The integration of the role-playing concept, which is also another time-consuming process, may lengthen the time used in the course and consequently increase the workloads of both participants and instructors.

Because of the aforementioned benefits and drawbacks, it can be summarized that the integration of the role-playing concept into IT-based BSGs is possible and also beneficent. However, while the problems mentioned above persist, thorough considerations have to be taken to determine whether the additional benefits can compensate the severed issues or to find solutions that can overcome the issues.

4.2 Potential technologies for IT-based business simulation games

In the following sections, the potential of two technologies, real-time data and dialog systems, will be discussed. The structure in each section will be similar to those of the previous sections. However, since the subject matters are not stand-alone concepts as in the case of serious game and role-playing, the process of assessing if they can be used in IT-based BSGs should also be different. The first parts of will still introduce the corresponding technologies by providing their definition, architecture and general usage. Meanwhile, the second parts will discusses in which part of the architecture of IT-based BSGs the technology can be integrated. In the last parts, the particular cases when the technology may be helpful, as well as the associating benefits and issues will also be mentioned.

4.2.1 The real-time data technology

With the increase of computer and Internet technology, the use of real-time data in information systems has been increasingly mentioned in the literature. However, in terms of education and training and especially in terms of business simulation games, there has been almost no work conducted to assess the potential of real-time data in this area.

As already mentioned above, firstly, an introduction to real-time data and its current usages will be provided in 4.3.1. Afterwards, section 4.3.2 will focus on how this technology can be integrated into IT-based BSGs while section 4.3.3 will mention the usage, benefits and issues of the integration.

4.2.1.1 Introduction to the real-time data technology

In the literature, real-time data are commonly mentioned within an overarching term of "real-time database system", which contains two aspects, data and data transaction (cf. Ramamritham 1993, p. 203 f.).

In terms of data, Ramamritham (1993, p. 203 f.) stated that real-time data have to be both logically and temporally consistent. While the satisfaction of the integrity constraints within a database can ensure the logical consistency of data, temporal consistency is more complex and consists of absolute consistency and relative consistency. In absolute consistency, the difference between the current time and the time when data were last collected has to be smaller than or equal to a predefined value. This consistency is expressed in the form of real-time constraints and deadlines. With relative consistency, the time between the collections of data sets, that are used to derive other data, also have to satisfy a time constraint.

Beside data, a database system also includes the transactions of data. Real-time database systems utilize all three types of database transactions: write-only transactions to write data on the database, upgrade transactions to renew data and read-only transactions to read data from the databases. All three types of data are also put under real-time constraints.

There are hard, soft and firm real-time constraints, based on the validity of data and the functionality of the whole system after the deadline is missed (cf. Liu et al. 2006, p. 320).

- Hard constraint: the exceeding of the deadline may result in failure of the system and the immediate loss in validity of the data. For that reason, no deadline miss is tolerated.

- Soft constraint: in this case, occasional misses are tolerable. After the deadline is missed, data will still be used to finish the task but with reduced value.

- Firm constraint: infrequent misses are also tolerable. However, the current task and data will be discarded while the system will continue to function.

Kopetz (2011, p. 22 ff.) gave several examples for systems that require the collection and processing of real-time data. The examples include a system that controls the flow of a liquid in a pipe and has to turn off the control valve immediately when the temperature of the liquid reaches a certain level. Another example is a system used for automobile engine that calculates the exact amount of fuel and the exact moment, in which the fuel has to be injected into the engine. It can be derived from the examples that the usage of real-time data and generally real-time computing is critical to systems that need to react quickly to changes in the environment.

In the literature on education and training, only few have made mentions of the usage of real-time data. The few examples that have been attended up until now include scientific simulations used in medical education or science, which collect or generate real-time data for training, as in the case of medical education, or for teaching and researching on scientific topics.

4.2.1.2 Real-time data and IT-based business simulation games

In order to assess how real-time data can be integrated into IT-based business simulation game, first, one has to identify what kind of data is needed in the architecture of business simulation game.

Section 2.4 described a general architecture of business simulation proposed by Hall (2012). The architecture shows four databases: the help database, the reporting database, the comments database and the parameter database. In the help database, help data for the use of the game are stored. The reporting database stores data that are used by the reporting engine to define the structure and contents of system feedbacks. The comments database is used to create comments on users' decisions, inputs and results. In the parameter database, data and parameters that are used for the calculations in the simulation model are stored. These data can also be transferred to the hypertext help engine to create help data, which provide learners with necessary information for their decision-making. Among the four databases, the help database, reporting database and comments database are static. Only the parameter database is dynamic and shows a potential for real-time data.

For that reason, if necessary, the normal parameter database in the architecture of IT-based BSGs can be replaced with a real-time database. Real-time data can be collected from the outside world or from the system and written into the database. After that, the data will be transferred to other components of the architecture to be used. For example, in a stock market simulation game, a real-time database system acting at the role of the parameter database can extract real-time stock prices and macroeconomic data from the real world or from a data generator that can create fictive stock prices for the use of the game. These data can be displayed to users to help them in their decision-making and will also be used by the simulation model in combination with users' decisions to calculate the results. After the calculation, data on the situation of the users will be actualized. All the transactions mentioned in the example, including the extraction of stock prices, the update of stock price data within the database, the display of data to users and the execution of users' decision must also satisfy the real-time constraints given by the developers.

4.2.1.3 Usage, benefits and issues

In practice, both the process of deploying IT-based BSGs and the games can be distinguished based on the pace of game play. There are turn-based and real-time BSGs. The more commonly used turn-based games are conducted in rounds with deadlines for participants to submit their decisions so that the simulation model can calculate them. Between the deadlines, the time, which is represented in the games, stops and no calculation takes place in the simulation model. Since no calculation takes place, there is no need to actualize the data stored in the database continuously between the deadlines. For that reason, it can be assumed that this type of BSGs does not need real-time data and the accompanying abilities and benefits. However, this is different in real-time BSGs. In real-time games, game play is continuous and participants have to react to the continuously changing situation in the game. In order to ensure this, the collection and procession of data from users, from the outside world or from data generators have to be finished within a predefined period of time, which is the prerequisite for the use of real-time data.

By using real-time data and real-time IT-based BSGs, the games put a harder time constraint on the reaction of participants in a continuous game play. This type of game play will consequently train them for "multi-tasking in a dynamic, real time and event driven leadership environment" (Corsi et al. 2006, p. 63). Moreover, real-time data could also increase the realism of the games and might increase the motivation and seriousness of participants.

Beside the aforementioned issue concerning the right usage case of the integration, no other issue that may accompany the integration can be sighted, except from technical issues relating to the development and management of real-time database systems. Thus, for the real-time data technology, it can be summarized that this technology can be integrated with positive effects into IT-based BSGs. However, the usage of this integration should be limited only to real-time game play.

4.2.2 The dialog system technology

Similar to real-time data, dialog systems use natural language processing (NLP) and voice recognition (VR), which are modern technologies, and can potentially enhance the performance of IT-based BSGs. Both technologies were suggested for BSGs by Summers (2004, p. 220) and was later suggested again by Bell et al. (2008, p. 1422) and Faria et al. (2009, p. 470). However, up until now, there has been almost no research taken to study the potentials of these technologies particularly to IT-based BSGs. This gives the reason for choosing these technologies as one of the focus points of this thesis.

In this section, dialog systems and the two technologies will be introduced along with their actual usage. Then, the potential of integrating these technologies into IT-based BSGs will be discussed. Subsequently a concrete method of integrating and using dialog systems will be suggested and the accompanying issues will also be studied.

4.2.2.1 Introduction to the dialog system technology

By definition, a dialog system is a system capable of interacting with human, using the language they understand, the natural language (cf. Morge et al. 2011, p. 142). Based on the modality of the interaction, it can be distinguished between text-based, which utilizes only NLP to allow learners to communicate with the system by typing a sentence, and spoken dialog system, which uses VR to allow for verbal interaction with the system. A classical architecture of a spoken dialog system, which not only uses VR to receive and understand human speech but can also generate spoken answers, is shown in the following figure.

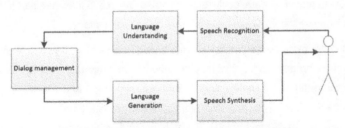

Figure 8: A classical architecture of a dialog system

Source: based on Bohus/Rudnicky (2009)

At the outermost layer of the architecture are the voice recognition and voice synthesis components, which, correspondingly, analyze the input voice or synthesize the output voice. In text-based dialog systems, these components are replaced with a user interface to receive user inputs and display system responds in the form of text. The results will then be sent to the language understanding component. This component has the objective of understanding the analyzed inputs by using linguistic analysis techniques. The analysis process starts at the word level, which leads to the meaning of the combination of words in a sentence and the meaning of the whole sentence with regard to the context of usage and knowledge about the outside world (cf. Liddy 1998, p. 138 f.). After understanding the inputs, this component extracts the required data and assigns them to predefined variables. The innermost component of the dialog systems is the dialog manager, which processes the variables received from the language understanding component and generate appropriate system responds in forms of instructions. The responds will then be passed to the language generator to create suitable sentences, which will lastly be sent to the speech synthesis to be transformed into speech and transmitted to users.

Dialog systems are currently applied in a wide range of applications, where human-machine interaction can replace human-human interaction. Examples includes applications that receive and answer customers' phone calls in a call-center, answer customers' queries on a product in text or speech in a website, help passengers navigate in public transportations or carry out telephone banking orders (cf. Chai et al. 2002, p. 64). The Siri application in Apple's devices is also among the newest examples of dialog system. In education and training, dialog systems are used in various applications to provide tutoring, question-answering, conversation practice for language learners, pedagogical agents and learning companions and dialogs to promote reflection and meta-cognitive skills (cf. Kerly et al. 2009, p. 169).

4.2.2.2 Dialog systems and IT-based business simulation games

In the standard architecture of IT-based BSGs introduced in section 2.4, the component that directly controls the interaction between human players and the system is the simulation manager. This component is the first to receive input from users, which is commonly in the form of text typed into input fields or predefined, selectable instructions and send them to the simulation model to be calculated. It also receives responds from the simulation model and controls which data will be displayed to customer while the display engine controls how the data will be displayed. Comparing the role of the simulation manager and the dialog manager of the dialog systems given in the previous section, there is a clear similarity. As a result, it is possible to suggest a method to expand the architecture of IT-based BSGs of Hall (2012) and integrate the dialog systems into it. The affected components are showed in the following figure.

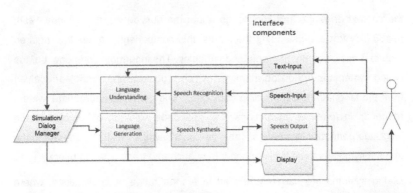

Figure 9: A propositional integration of dialog systems into the architecture of IT-based business simulation games

An expansion of the architecture will provide IT-based BSGs with the ability to receive input and respond in both text and speech. In case of text input, if the inputs are submitted via input fields, they can be assigned into variables and directly sent to the simulation/dialog manager. However, if text inputs are submitted in the form of sentences, they have to be sent to the language understanding component first so that the required data can be extracted from the sentences and forwarded to the simulation/dialog manager. Speech inputs are handled by the speech recognition component as in the architecture of dialog systems described above. The system can display outputs in the form of text directly or send them to the language generation component to create sentences. Like speech inputs, the processing of text outputs remains unchanged. A graphical user interface is responsible for receiving user inputs and displaying, as well as transmitting system responds.

4.2.2.3 Usage, benefits and issues

In spite of the proposed integration method, the actual usage of dialog systems in the gaming process still has to be attended. As already mentioned, dialog systems can be used where human-machine interaction takes place and replaces human-human interaction. In the gaming process introduced in section 2.3, there are several places where human-machine interaction can happen. For instance, dialog systems can be applied in the form of question-answering in the briefing phase, when participants have to learn about the simulation game and obtain basic knowledge required for the game. During game play, dialog systems can be used to provide participants with instructions and helps when needed. In the debriefing phase, commonly, participants make careful reflection on their behaviors and performance with the help of the instructors. In this phase, dialog systems can also be applied in the form of question-answering to help learners reflecting on their behaviors and performance.

When used as described above, dialog systems can bring benefits to the participants and the instructors of the BSGs. For instructors, the replacement of human-human interaction by human-machine interaction at some points of the business gaming process might reduce the workload of human instructors and may proceed to the complete replacement of human instructors. In the usage case described above, well-developed dialog systems embedded in BSGs can conduct and accomplish the objectives of human instructors such as introducing participants to the game, providing instructions and helps during game play and facilitating debriefing at the end of the game. Moreover, they can occasionally outperform human instructors (cf. Graesser et al. 2004, p. 189). For participants, the integration might improve their learning. Like simulation gaming, the use of conversations in the form of both text and speech promote active participation from the side of leaners. The active participation, stiffened by the novelty of the technology, can increase learners' motivation (cf. by Kerly et al. 2009, p. 169). Secondly, the use of dialog systems as a replacement for human instructors also helps decentralizing the learning process and gives learners more flexibility in learning. In particular, learners do not need to be present at the class to receive information of instructors or to contact them for instructions and helps. These objectives can be accomplished by the dialog systems. The benefits in motivation and flexibility can indirectly increase the learning outcomes. Directly, the use of dialogs and conversations in the process of knowledge transferring, such as in the briefing and debriefing phases, can improve learners' knowledge gain and retention. This has been confirmed by the study of Graesser et al. (2004, p. 189) that the use of dialog systems "is effective in promoting is effective in promoting learning gains at deep levels of comprehension".

Beside the promising benefits, the integration also shows some limitations. Although dialog systems may potentially replace human instructors, there are also several tasks that machines might not be able to solve, especially those relating to emotions. For example, instructors have to recognize and take proper measurements to prevent socio-emotional problems during competitive game play, in which inferior participants might be so frustrated and discouraged that they fail to continue the game (cf. Hofstede et al. 2010, p. 839 f.). However, the recognition of human emotions only by analyzing speech is not a simple task for machines. This issue limits the use of dialog systems only as a complementary tool for human instructors or in cases, in which human instructors are normally not required, such as in individually played BSGs. Furthermore, since dialog system is a new and complex technology, there might be problems concerning the novelty of the technology such as the unfamiliar with the technique of both learners and facilitators and the quality and complexity of the whole system. Last but not less importantly, the additional cost and complexity in relation with the development and deployment of dialog-enhanced IT-based BSGs also have to be taken into account when considering the integration and use of dialog systems in IT-based business simulation game.

To conclude this section, it can be asserted that the dialog system technology is a potential enhancement for IT-based BSGs because of the benefits it can contribute. Due to some limitations, the technology cannot completely replace human instructors. However, other temporary limitations concerning the novelty of the technology can be gradually overcome with the advancement of information technology.

5. Discussion

Throughout their development history, IT-based business simulation games have established firm domains of application. With the general target of motivating participants and engage them in a realistic gaming and learning process, IT-based BSGs are currently used in three main application fields. They are education and training, experimental research and business practice. In each of the application fields, there are different usage purposes focusing on specific domains. In education and training, IT-based BSGs are used to teach basic knowledge, provide deep understanding of the cross-functional relationships within a company and train technical, as well as social skills. Besides, specific research domains such as economics, organization and psychology are also using IT-based BSGs in their experimental researches. In business practice, there are reports of the use of IT-based BSGs as tools in strategic planning, employee assessment and recruitment.

As for the potentials for the future of IT-based BSGs, the fourth chapter has taken into account two concepts and two technologies. The serious game concept would be effective when used for the future generation of learners. However, issues such as a proper usage context and the unfamiliarity with the method of other groups of learners may hinder its effectiveness. The role-playing concept should be integrated to the simulation gaming process to enhance the effectiveness of courses that focusing on the training of interpersonal skills. The concepts also share some issues that have been found in IT-based BSGs and the integration may even severe them to some extents. The technology of real-time data can be integrated into the architecture of IT-based BSGs to increase the realism of the games. However, the actual usage of the integration is limited only to real-time BSGs, which are not a common type of BSGs. Dialog systems have shown their potentials for enhancing the human-machine interactions in IT-based BSGs, which consequently reduce the workload of instructors and improve learning outcomes. However, issues such as the irreplaceable roles of human instructors and again the unfamiliarity of learners can be mentioned.

This thesis is limited as a literature review to provide an overview on the current usage of IT-based BSGs. To demonstrate the results, deeper researches in the form of surveys can be conducted in the future to study the actual usage level of IT-based BSGs in each of the mentioned usage domains. Besides, because of the limitations in size and scope of the thesis, it was not possible to specialize into any of the potentials mentioned in this thesis. The suggestions and discussions provided in each of the potentials can be used as points of reference for deeper studies into each topic. In addition, the four potentials studied in this thesis have been exemplarily taken based on several selection criteria. Thus, they do not provide a complete list of the potentials. The advancements in computer technology and instructional methodology are still shaping the future of IT-based BSGs. Thus, in the future, the effects of emerging technologies and concepts on IT-based BSGs should be studies thoroughly and continuously.

Bibliography

(Abt 1987): Abt, C.C.: Serious games, Lanham, USA 1987.

(Anderson/Lawton 2009): Anderson, P.H.; Lawton, L.: Business simulations and cognitive learning: developments, desires and future directions. In: Simulation & Gaming 40 (2009) 2, pp. 193-216.

(Arias-Aranda/Bustinza-Sánchez 2009): Arias-Aranda, D.; Bustinza-Sánchez, O.: Entrepreneurial attitude and conflict management through business simulations. In: Industrial Management & Data Systems 109 (2009) 8, pp. 1101-1117.

(Baume 2009): Baume, M.: Computerunterstützte Planspiele für das Informationsmanagement: Realitätsnahe und praxisorientierte Ausbildung in der universitären Lehre am Beispiel der „CIO-Simulation", Norderstedt, Germany 2009.

(Bell et al. 2008): Bell, B.S.; Kanar, A.M.; Kozlowski, S.W.J.: Current issues and future directions in simulation-based training. In: International Journal of Human Resource Management 19 (2008) 8, pp. 1416-1434.

(Bernard/Cannon 2011): Bernard, R.R.S.; Cannon, H.M.: Exploring motivation: Using emoticons to map student motivation in a business game exercise. In: Developments in Business Simulation and Experiential Learning 38 (2011), pp. 229-240.

(Bielecki 1993): Bielecki, W.T.: DSS MANAGER: Turning business simulation into a decision support system. In: Journal of Management Development 12 (1993) 3, pp. 60-64.

(Blötz 2008): Blötz, U.: Planspiele in der beruflichen Bildung, 1st ed, Bielefeld, Germany 2008.

(Bohus/Rudnicky 2009): Bohus, D.; Rudnicky, A.I.: The RavenClaw dialog management framework: Architecture and systems. In: Computer Speech & Language 23 (2009) 3, pp. 332–361.

(Cannon-Bowers/Bowers 2008): Cannon-Bowers, J.A.; Bowers, C.A.: Synthetic learning environments. In: Spector, J.M.; Merrill, M.D.; van Merriënboer, J.; Driscoll, M.P. (eds): Handbook of research on educational communications and technology, 3rd ed, New York, USA 2008, pp. 317-327.

(CAPSIM 2012): CAPSIM: Management and Executive Training using Capsim business simulations. http://www.capsim.com/business-simulations/corporate/business-management-training.html, accessed on 2012-10-16.

(Chai et al. 2002): Chai, J.; Horvath, V.; Nicolov, N.; Stys, M.; Kambhatla, N.; Zadrozny, W.; Melville, P.: Natural language assistant: A dialog system for online product recommendation. In: AI Magazine 23 (2002) 2, pp. 63-75.

(Cohen/Rhenman 1961): Cohen, K.J.; Rhenman, E.: The role of management games in education and research. In: Management Science 7 (1961) 2, pp. 131-166.

(Corsi et al. 2006): Corsi, T.; Boyson, S.; van Houten, S.A.; Verbraeck, A.; Han, C.; Macdonald, J.R.: The real-time global supply chain game: New educational tool for developing supply chain management professionals. In: Transportation Journal 45 (2006) 3, pp. 61-73.

(Coutu 1951): Coutu, W.: Role-playing vs. Role-taking: An appeal for clarification. In: American Sociological Review 16 (1951) 2, pp. 180-187.

(Crookall 2010): Crookall, D.: Serious games, debriefing, and simulation/gaming as a discipline. In: Simulation & Gaming 41 (2010) 6, pp. 898-920.

(de Freitas 2006): de Freitas, S.: Learning in immersive worlds: A review of game-based learning. http://www.jisc.ac.uk/media/documents/programmes/elearninginnovatio n/gamingreport_v3.pdf, 2006, accessed on 2012-10-04.

(Faria 2001): Faria, A.J.: The changing nature of business simulation/ gaming research: A brief history. In: Simulation & Gaming 32 (2001) 1, pp. 97-110.

(Faria et al. 2009): Faria, A.J.; Hutchinson, D.; Wellington, W.J.; Gold, S.: Developments in business gaming: A review of the past 40 years. In: Simulation & Gaming 40 (2009) 4, pp. 464-487.

(Feinstein et al. 2002): Feinstein, A.H.; Mann, S.; Corsun, D.L.: Charting the experiential territory: Clarifying definitions and uses of computer simulation, games, and role play. In: Journal of Management Development 21 (2002) 10, pp. 732-744.

(Fripp 1997): Fripp, J.: A future for business simulations?. In: Journal of European Industrial Training 21 (1997) 4, pp. 138-142.

(Fritzsche/Cotter 1992): Fritzsche, D.J.; Cotter, R.V.: Benefits of internet computer networks for ABSEL members. In: Developments in Business Simulation & Experiential Exercises 19 (1992), pp. 51-53.

(Gardner et al. 2009): Gardner, L.L.; Gausman, L.C.; Silvers, K.J.: Recruiting the supply chain professionals of the future: A supply chain summer camp for middle school students. In: Decision Sciences Journal of Innovative Education 7 (2009) 1, pp. 221-232.

(Garris et al. 2002): Garris, R.; Ahlers, R.; Driskell, J. E.: Games, motivation, and learning: A research and practice model. In: Simulation & Gaming 33 (2002) 4, pp. 441-467.

(Graesser et al. 2004): Graesser, A.C.; Lu, S.; Jackson, G.T.; Mitchell, H.H.; Ventura, M.; Olney, A.; Louwerse, M.M.: AutoTutor: A tutor with dialogue in natural language. In: Behavior Research Methods, Instruments, & Computers 36 (2004) 2, pp. 180-192.

(Greenblat 1973): Greenblat, C.S.: Teaching with simulation games: A review of claims and evidence. In: Teaching Sociology 1 (1973) 1, pp. 62-83.

(Hall 2012): Hall, J.J.S.B.: Existing and emerging business simulation-game design movements. In: Developments in Business Simulation and Experiential Learning 36 (2009), pp. 132-136.

(Hall 2009): Hall, J.J.S.B.: Business Simulation software architecture. http://www.simulations.co.uk/DESIGN08.HTM, accessed on 2012-10-18.

(Hauke et al. 2005): Hauke, R., Baume, M.; Krcmar, H.: Kategorisierung von Planspielen: Entwicklung eines übergreifenden Strukturschemas zur Einordnung und Abgrenzung von Planspielen, Garching, Germany 2005.

(Hauke et al. 2006): Hauke, R., Baume, M.; Krcmar, H.: Computerunterstützte Management-Planspiele: Ergebnisse einer Untersuchung des Planspieleinsatzes in Unternehmen und Bildungseinrichtungen, Garching, Germany 2006.

(Hofstede et al. 2010): Hofstede, G.J.; de Caluwé, L.; Peters, V.: Why simulation games work – In search of the active substance: A synthesis. In: Simulation & Gaming 41 (2010) 6, pp. 824-843.

(Hottner 2007): Hottner, F.: Archiv – ACTA Allensbacher Computer- und Technik-Analyse. http://www.ifd-allensbach.de/fileadmin/ACTA/ACTA_Praesentationen/2007/ACTA2007_Hottner.pdf, accessed on 2012-10-05.

(Hsu 1989): Hsu, E.: Role-event gaming simulation in management education: A conceptual framework and review. In: Simulation & Gaming 20 (1989) 4, pp. 409-438.

(Karczewski 1990): Karczewski, S.: Die Entwicklung einer modularen Gesamtarchitektur für die Softwarekomponenten von Planspielen, Wiesbaden, Germany 1990.

(Kerly et al. 2009): Kerly, A.; Ellis, R.; Bull, S.: Conversational agents in E-Learning. In: Allen, T.; Ellis, R.; Petridis, M. (eds): Applications and Innovations in Intelligent Systems XVI, London, UK 2009, pp. 169-182.

(Kern 2003): Kern, M.: Planspiele im Internet – Netzbasierte Lernarrangements zur Vermittlung betriebswirtschaftlicher Kompetenz, 1st ed, Wiesbaden, Germany 2003.

(Keys/Wolfe 1990): Keys, J.B.; Wolfe, J.: The role of management games and simulations in education and research. In: Journal of Management 16 (1990) 2, pp. 307-336.

(Keys/Biggs 1990): Keys, J.B.; Biggs, W.D.: A review of business games. In: Gentry, J.W. (ed): Guide to business gaming and experiential learning, East Brunswick, USA 1990, pp. 48-73.

(Kopetz 2011): Kopetz, H.: Real-Time Systems: Design Principles for Distributed Embedded Applications, 2nd ed, New York, USA 2011.

(Kozlowski/Bell 2007): Kozlowski, S.W.J.; Bell, B.S.: A theory-based approach for designing distributed learning systems. In: Fiore, S.M.; Salas, E. (eds): Toward a science of distributed learning, Washington, DC, USA 2007, pp. 15-39.

(Kraiger et al. 1993): Kraiger, K.; Ford, J.K.; Salas, E.: Application of cognitive, skill-based and affective theories of learning outcomes to new methods of training evaluation. In: Journal of Applied Psychology 78 (1993) 2, pp. 311-328.

(Léger 2006): Léger, P.-M.: Using a simulation game approach to teach Enterprise Resource Planning concepts, Montréal, Canada 2006.

(Liddy 1998): Liddy, E.D.: Natural language processing for information retrieval and knowledge discovery. In: Cochrane, P.A.; Johnson, E.H. (eds): Visualizing Subject Access for 21st Century Information Resources, Urbana-Champaign, USA 1998, pp. 137-147.

(Linser 2011): Linser, R.: Role rules!!! Roles and rules in role based e-learning. In: Proceedings of The 2011 New Orleans International Academic Conference, New Orleans, USA 2011, pp. 907-913.

(Liu et al. 2006): Liu, D.; Hu, X.S.; Lemmon, M.D.; Ling, Q.: Firm real-time system scheduling based on a novel QoS constraint. In: IEEE Transactions on Computers 55 (2006) 3, pp. 320-333.

(Micheal/Chen 2006): Micheal, D.; Chen, S.: Serious games: Games that educate, train and inform, 1st ed, Boston, USA 2006.

(Micklich 1998): Micklich, D.L.: The 'Class Approach' in behavioral simulation in a business policy/strategic management course: A progression toward greater realism. In: Developments in Business Simulation and Experiential Learning 25 (1998), pp. 90-91.

(Morge et al. 2011): Morge, M.; Abdel-Naby, S.; Beaufils, B.: Towards a dialectical approach for conversational agents in selling situations. In: McBurney, P.; Rahwan, I.; Parsons, S. (eds): Argumentation in Multi-Agent Systems, Heidelberg, Germany 2011, pp. 141-158.

(NoviCraft 2012): NoviCraft: Learning path is simple| NoviCraft – Serious Game for team building and leadership training by TeamStream. http://www.novicraft.com/en/learning-path-simple, accessed on 2012-10-04.

(Orth 1997): Orth, C.: Unternehmensplanspiele in der betriebswirtschaftliche Aus- und Weiterbildung, Göttingen, Germany 1997.

(Pivec et al. 2003): Pivec, M.; Dziabenko, O.; Schinnerl, I.: Aspects of game-based learning. In: Proceedings of I-KNOW '03, Graz, Austria 2003, pp. 216-225.

(Pomper et al. 2009): Pomper, A., Jordaan, B.; Ravesloot, J.: The added value of serious games in management development programs: The Slowesa case. In: PMI Global Congress 2009 – EMEA, 2009-05-18 to 2009-05-20, Amsterdam, Netherlands 2009.

(Prensky 2001): Prensky, M.: Digital Game-Based Learning, New York, USA 2001.

(Proserpio/Gioia 2007): Proserpio, L.; Gioia, D.A.: Teaching the virtual generation. In: Academy of Management Learning & Education 6 (2007) 1, pp. 69-80.

(Rainey/Lawlor-Wright 2011): Rainey, M.J.; Lawlor-Wright, T.F.: Student perspectives on communication: a case study on different methods of communication used by engineering students. In: European Conference on Civil Engineering Education and Training, 2011-11-24 to 2011-11-26, Patras, Greece 2011.

(Ramamritham 1993): Ramamritham, K.: Real-time databases. In: Distributed and Parallel Databases 1 (1993), pp. 199-226.

(Randel et al. 1993): Randel, J.M.; Morris, B.A.; Wetzel, C.D.; Whitehill, B.V.: The effectiveness of games for educational purposes: A review of recent research. In: Simulation & Gaming 23 (1993) 3, pp. 261-276.

(Sauaia/Kallás 2003): Sauaia, A.C.A.; Kallás, D.: Cooperate for profits or compete for market? Study of oligopolistic pricing with a business game. In: Developments in Business Simulation and Experiential Learning, 30 (2003), pp. 232-242.

(Siewiorek/Lehtinen 2011): Siewiorek, A.; Lehtinen, E.: Exploring leadership profiles from collaborative computer gaming. In: International Journal of Leadership Studies 6 (2011) 3, pp. 357-374.

(Simulated Training Systems 2012): Simulated Training Systems: Digital Game Based Learning (DGBL). http://www.simulatedtrainingsystems.com/cas eStudy.htm, accessed on 2012-10-04.

(Sitzmann 2011): Sitzmann, T.: A meta-analytic examination of the instructional effectiveness of computer-based simulation games. In: Personnel Psychology 64 (2011), pp. 489-528.

(Smed/Hakonen 2003): Smed, J.; Hakonen, H.: Towards a definition of a computer game, Turku, Finland 2003.

(Sogunro 2004): Sogunro, O.A.: Efficacy of role-playing pedagogy in training leaders: Some reflections. In: Journal of Management Development 23 (2004) 4, pp. 355-371.

(StratX 2012): StratX: Markstrat. http://www.stratxsimulations.com/markstrat_on line_home.aspx, accessed on 2012-10-02.

(Summers 2004): Summers, G.J.: Today's business simulation industry. In: Simulation & Gaming 35 (2004) 2, pp. 208-241.

(Tennyson/Jorczak 2008): Tennyson, R.D.; Jorczak, R.L.: A conceptual framework for the empirical study of instructional games. In: O'Neil, H.F.; Perez, R.S. (eds): Computer games and team and individual learning, Oxford, UK 2008, pp. 39-54.

(Thiagarajan 1996): Thiagarajan, S.: Instructional games, simulations, and role-plays. In: Craig, R.L. (ed): The ASTD Training and Development Handbook, 4th ed, New York, USA 1996, pp. 517-533.

(Thornton/Cleveland 1990): Thornton, G.C.; Cleveland, J.N.: Developing managerial talent through simulation. In: American Psychologist 45 (1990) 2, pp. 190-199.

(TOPSIM 2012): TOPSIM: Learning business by doing business: TOPSIM General Management. http://www.topsim.com/fileadmin/data/Download

s_TOPSIM/TOPSIM_General_Management_KB.pdf, accessed on 2012-10-02.

(van Ments 1983): van Ments, M.: The effective use of role-play: A handbook for teachers and trainers, 1st ed, London, UK 1983.

(Wawer et al. 2010): Wawer, M.; Milosz, M.; Muryjas, P.; Rzemieniak, M.: Business simulation games in forming of students' entrepreneurship. In: International Journal of Euro-Mediterranean Studies 3 (2010) 1, pp. 49-71.

(Wellington/Faria 1991): Wellington, W.J.; Faria, A.J.: An investigation of the relationship between simulation play, performance level and recency of play on exam scores. In: Developments in Business Simulation & Experiential Exercises 18 (1991), pp. 111-114.

(Whitton/Hynes 2006): Whitton, N.; Hynes, N.: Evaluating the effectiveness of an online simulation to teach business skills. http://www.ascilite.org.au/a jet/e-jist/docs/vol9_no1/papers/current_practice/whitton_hynes.htm, 2006, accessed on 2012-11-08.

(Wills/McDougall 2009): Wills, S.; McDougall, A.: Reusability of online role play as learning objects or learning designs. In: Lockyer, L.; Bennett, S.; Agostinho, S.; Harper, B. (eds): Handbook of research on learning design and learning objects: Issues, applications and technologies, Hershey, USA 2009, pp. 761-776.

(Wilson et al. 2009): Wilson, K.A.; Bedwell, W.L.; Lazzara, E.H.; Salas, E.; Burke, C.S.; Estock, J.L.; Orvis, K.L.; Conkey, C.: Relationships between game attributes and learning outcomes: Reviews and research proposals. In: Simulation & Gaming 40 (2009) 2, pp. 217-266.

(Wong et al. 2007): Wong, W.L.; Shen, C.; Nocera, L.; Carriazo, E.; Tang, F.; Bugga, S.; Narayanan, H.; Wang, H.; Ritterfeld, U.: Serious video game effectiveness. In: Proceedings of the international conference on Advances in computer entertainment technology ACE 07, New York, USA 2007, pp. 49-55.